The Keep Calm Guy

Change Leadership

How to lead people through change

Bill Mann

III Clink
Street

London | New York

Published by Clink Street Publishing 2019

Copyright © 2019

First edition.

ISBN:
978-1-913340-39-1 paperback
978-1-913340-40-7 ebook

What people are saying

What people are saying about the author, and his previous book *How to Keep Calm and Carry On*, which describes how to successfully face change from a personal perspective:

"A book to keep and return to for ongoing guidance and insight. Well worth the read."

"I'd 100% recommend this book for anyone undergoing major changes in their lives."

"As a life coach I am always looking for helpful books to recommend to my clients... I recommend this excellent little book."

"A life affirming book... I would strongly recommend to anyone experiencing change, no matter how small."

"Wow – what a read!"

"This book is one to read start to finish, and easy to dip in and out of as future reference."

"A book to keep and return to for ongoing guidance and insight. Well worth the read."

This book is dedicated to my wife, Sarah,
for her unconditional love and support

Contents

Preface   1

Introduction   5

Part 1: Change & Transformation   13
   People First   15
   Organisational Changes   21
   The Challenges   35
   The Resistance   43
   Consequences   49
   The Prize – Getting It Right   55

Part 2: Emotional Intelligence   63
   Emotional Intelligence   65
   12 EI Traits and Behaviours   71
   EI in the Workplace   81

Part 3: Applying It   97
   Psychology of Change   99
   Leading Change with EI   107
   Beyond EI   115
   Leadership Support   121

Part 4: The Way Forward   **127**
    A Letter to You   129
    The Real Transformation   137
    Next Steps   141
    The Keep Calm Guy   147
    Recommend Reading   151

About the Author   **153**

Acknowledgements   **155**

Preface

Organisations are constantly changing. It could be something small such as a change to a single team or individual, or a change to working processes. It may be something larger such as a restructure or reorganisation. It may even be something all-encompassing such as a merger, acquisition, or a full-scale transformation programme. Whatever it is, changes are commonplace – but they all usually miss one vital ingredient. Formal Change Management processes will ensure the analysis is done, designs completed, and implementation plans are executed. They will even include communication plans and mapping of roles and resources. All that is missing is the most important component – winning the hearts and minds of the people involved so they are fully committed to making it happen. Without this there will be resistance. And if the resistance is not overcome, the change programme will fail.

Change can be imposed – but it is a costly, painful, and naïve approach. Losing key resources and the drain on management time alone is to be avoided. Treating staff as people rather than resources, managing impacts with humanity, and managing relationships with emotional intelligence, will deliver results, respect, and loyalty that will long outlive the change project. By securing the full commitment of everyone involved change can be made quickly and with ease.

If you have picked up this book the chances are you are facing change in your organisation, or perhaps you are the one leading the change. Either way it isn't easy. Whether it is a full-scale reorganisation, perhaps as the result of a merger or acquisition, or simply redeploying individuals where the business needs it, getting the buy-in and support of all involved is difficult for even the most enlightened leaders. Even routine activities such as managing a pay review can stir up a tidal wave of emotions if not handled with care. The consequences of simply imposing change can lead to months of lost productivity, damage to morale and motivation, and ultimately impacts customer service and delivery. All of this can be mitigated if not avoided by skilful handling and the use of emotional intelligence. Getting it right can save businesses a fortune in management time, recruitment fees, and lost productivity. It can avoid damaging relationships and trust. Add to that the motivation of an engaged and loyal workforce and the benefits last for many years.

When we go to work and enter the office door we put on our professional persona and adopt the role we were slotted in to. Yet we cannot separate this from who we are as a person and neither can our colleagues or staff. To manage change purely in the context of the business structure and professional roles is to deny the fact we are dealing with people with deeply personal cares and worries, and missing the key ingredient to managing change successfully.

Bill Mann has spent a long career in businesses of vastly different sizes and in many different countries. He has managed change from the individual all the way through to

M&A scale restructuring. He has seen it all. In this book he explains the critical ingredient to success, often overlooked by many – keeping staff fully engaged all the way through the process. The pain that usually accompanies major change – the uncertainty, dip in morale and productivity, loss of key people, and inevitable impact on customer service, can be avoided with skilful handling.

On the 7th July 2005 Bill was caught up in the London bombings when he was in the carriage of the Circle Line train at Edgware Road that was targeted by a suicide bomber. He was fortunate to escape with his life, but little did he know that it would never be the same again. A few years later he was still grappling with the aftereffects of this trauma when his wife was diagnosed with breast cancer. Left alone to bring up his young family Bill's life was turned upside down. It is testament to his inner strength and emotional intelligence that he, and his family, came through this period of his life successfully. Bill has learnt a lot about change – the hard way, and it is described with a refreshing honesty and clarity in his previous book *How to Keep Calm and Carry On*.

In this book Bill shows us we can use emotional intelligence to lead any size of change in business. Unfortunately, in many organisations change is implemented by simply being imposed – a blunt instrument that has many unintended consequences. With the tools, techniques, and behaviours described in the following chapters the same change, no matter how unpalatable to some staff, can be made with the minimum of disruption, but also with care, empathy, and understanding. I recommend it to any executive or manager responsible for making change in their organisation, or anyone simply wishing to develop their emotional intelligence.

Introduction

It's the smells and sounds that stay with you. The taste of soot and smoke engulfed my senses for days, weeks and months afterwards. The sounds, of fear, distress, unimaginable pain and pure terror, became the soundtrack for my nightmares.

My name is Bill Mann and on July 7th, 2005, I boarded a Circle Line London Underground train to Paddington. It was normal day for me. Balmy by the dubious standards of the English summer, so an uncomfortable commute lay ahead on London's bustling transport network, but my thoughts were on the day ahead. Meetings, specific jobs in the office in Paddington.

I'd said my usual goodbyes to my wife and children and set off for London Fenchurch Street, before wandering around the corner to Tower Hill underground station. I stood on the platform in the same spot I always did despite the rush hour. When the train came to a screeching halt, I boarded the same carriage I always did. A creature of habit, perhaps, but perfect for a quick exit at the other end.

The train rolled into Edgware Road. I'd occasionally disembark there and enjoy a walk into Paddington. I don't know why I didn't that day. If only I had.

I wouldn't describe myself as a people watcher on the Tube. Many are. Some are happy with their thoughts, like me, while others read the morning papers and most, in this digital age, are engrossed in their phones and tablets. I sat contemplating the day ahead as the train moved into the tunnel away from the Edgware Road platform.

A train passed beside us in the opposite direction as I was thrown from my seat towards the doors. The flash of light was blinding and the intensity of the heat scolded my skin which was already damp with sweat. The darkness was illuminated only by the emergency lighting in the tunnel and the burning embers that flashed past me. The screeching sound of metal on metal was only later drowned out by the screams that would haunt me.

They say your life flashes before you when you are so close to death and it is true. But a need to survive and pure instinct is what saved me that day, the day London had feared since the horrors of 9/11.

I waited for the impact that would surely end my life but it didn't come. The fireball that I thought would sweep through the carriage did not come. As the train ground to a halt, there was silence. After that, panic.

Fragments of broken glass showered down on me. I put out my hand and managed to grab a hand-rail to break my fall. Slowly, as people surveyed the situation, all those who were able to started to help the injured and the dying. Passengers in the passing train looked through their windows in horror. Some broke windows and passed in bottles or water or climbed through to help. Some people had been blown out of the carriage by the force of the bomb and others jumped down to help them.

The evacuation had started but I stayed to help. The emergency services arrived faced with their worst nightmare, and I will never forget the words of the paramedic that first walked through and assessed the situation with his colleagues: "Five fatalities and five seriously injured."

I was one of the lucky ones that was able to walk out the carriage unaided. Shock cripples you in the moments when you need your strength most; I struggled to walk to the end of the train and down a ladder on to the tracks and out of the station.

The man that emerged into the warm air of North London was very different to the one that had boarded the train just minutes earlier. My life had changed in an instant. My priorities were turned upside down and my perspective permanently changed. For a moment the only thing that mattered was life over death. The thoughts that had dominated my morning were redundant. Thoughts of the things I had to do at work vanished. Thoughts of other things that were once important vanished into the background. Bills to pay, the mortgage, house to renovate, cars to run, job security. They suddenly became unworthy of the worry and stress that they once taken. Life and health were the only need, and still are.

Outside of the station we were shepherded into the local branch of Marks & Spencer where staff were providing chairs and water, before we were moved over the road to the Hilton Metropole Hotel where ambulance staff and paramedics assessed the injured. Being one of the least injured, I was in the final tranche of people taken to the Royal Free Hospital in Hampstead.

Although covered in blood from people I had tried to assist, my only physical injury was blast damage to my eardrums and a few minor cuts and scratches. I was rather bemused when the doctor said I was free to go home. I was on the wrong side of London, and the whole transport network was shut down.

Eventually, I was able to find a mini-cab. The driver was an immigrant from Afghanistan who had lost several family members in similar circumstances. He was one of the few people I have spoken to who has any understanding of the trauma. Eventually, I made it home. The house was empty, and I showered off the blood and grime. I showered again to get clean, but didn't feel it. My clothes went straight into a black sack and were put outside the back door. The children walked in from school later that afternoon and wondered why their dad was home early from work.

Such a profound change took years to adjust to and to accept. This was a major trauma that only others that had been through a similar event could comprehend. Indeed, it was only when I met a victim of a similar terrorist bombing that I was able to move forward. It was a trauma that I largely had to deal with myself as others could not relate to. The questions were endless. Why? Why me? What if I had sat a few seats further up? What if I had entered a different set of doors? Why that train and not the one earlier or later? What if I had got off at Edgware Road? So many questions but no answers. What next? Do I go back to work and do that journey again every day? Do I let it change my life by having to change job and not commute? Why should it? Why should I let the terrorists win? More and more questions. Fewer and fewer answers.

I decided I had to get back in the saddle and do the journey again and not be defeated. I could not give up a good job. I could not stop visiting London when I lived on its doorstep. I could not have my life compromised so severely. The decision was not just a practical one. It was a choice of falling to pieces or facing up to reality and getting on with life. I felt on the edge – I could easily have gone either way. In the days and weeks that followed more and more individual stories came out and I could understand and sympathise with them all.

Going back to work, I had very refreshing clarity regarding my inbox and to-do list. None of it was of any consequence. Not to say that none of it was important, or even that others would not view it as extremely important or critical to the business. My frame of reference had changed. Never before had the value of life been so profound, or the fragility of life been so scary. Every day was something to give thanks for and every day was an opportunity to cherish and take advantage of. This new perspective was both a blessing and a curse. How could I be motivated by a presentation deck to be delivered to a committee for approval? How could I consider writing a report as a good use of the precious hours I had in my day? Motivation to make the most of each and every day was very strong and something I have tried to retain. Motivation to deal with things of little or no consequence against my new frame of reference was a struggle.

I felt I was just getting my head above water and coming to terms with what happened when my wife, my life partner since we were both 17, was diagnosed with cancer. A few years later, it returned, and this time it was terminal. This time it was not just myself but our children I had to help through this tragedy.

Yet again my life, our life, was turned upside down. Perspectives changed, priorities changed, and our futures changed. Without doubt my experience of dealing with the personal impacts of surviving the bomb helped me get through this period. I knew the mental strength was there that I could draw on. I knew the self-defence mechanisms were there that I could rely on. I knew I had the tools and techniques to help me cope and process this most drastic and brutal change to our lives. It is not without pride that I look back at how successful this has been, and how I have been able to guide the children through it, to become happy and well-balanced young adults. It could have been so different.

Before both of these events, and since then, there have been other changes I have had to face that are far more common. Both positive and negative, planned and unexpected. The sort of changes that many people face during their lives: starting a new job, losing a job, moving house, starting relationships, having children, ending relationships, and so on. We all face change on a day-to-day basis. Events change our plans for the days or weeks ahead, whether it be a cancelled appointment, travel delays, unexpected visitors, etc. All of these things are a change and they can all invoke the same set of emotions and turmoil, albeit on a smaller scale. How many people get frustrated or even angry if their plans for the day are changed, even if it cannot be helped? Sometimes, these minor daily irritations can change our outlook on the whole day or even longer. They all require us to process the change and make decisions about how we move forward. The scale may be different, but it is fundamentally the same process we go through.

I am not here to judge, nor to say my experience of 7/7 and my wife's death mean those, whose plans have been ruined simply don't match up to what I have been through. Far from it, change is relative and how you deal with it can make you or break you, regardless of the scale of the event.

My earlier experiences have certainly helped me keep those smaller scale changes in perspective and allowed me to accept and adapt to them much easier than I would have in the past. But even looking back before the bomb I can recognise in myself an ability to keep a cool head in the face of change and not be phased by events that others struggle with, the ability to 'Keep Calm and Carry On'.

These two events were clearly life changing. As I considered my return to work and my future career, I had renewed empathy for people that were struggling with change in the workplace. I could suddenly see with absolute clarity why people facing possible redundancy, or a new role, new line manager, new location, etc were reacting with such strong emotions and resisting the changes.

As I reflected on the numerous organisational changes I have had been through, as well as the one I was currently facing, it became painfully obvious that the complete disconnect between organisational change and personal change is the reason why many change projects fail. This is a situation that is being repeated every day across many, many, businesses. Yet it is something that is incredibly easy to fix with a little empathy and kindness.

Part 1:
Change & Transformation

So how did the rest of the team take the news of your promotion?

*"Remember, the only constant
in life is change."*
– Buddha

People First

*Every business is constantly changing – or should be if it
expects to survive, and it is the people in the organisation that
have to make the change. The benefits of learning how to lead
change with emotional intelligence and avoid the resistance
and fall out that often goes with change are priceless.*

Businesses of all sizes, and across every industry, are constantly changing. It may be organically by growing or evolving products and services, or maturing and optimising, or possibly even declining and downsizing. It may be by specific actions such as a merger or acquisition, or a reorganisation, relocation, or simply by recruiting and moving staff to new positions. It may be something seemingly small such as changing the reporting lines of one individual, or something that affects the entire organisation. It could even be something routine such as an annual performance appraisal and pay review. Whatever the reason no business stands still – change is constant.

Walk into any business with more than a handful of staff and there will be change planned, being made, or people struggling with the unintended consequences of change. Structures will change, people are promoted, moved in to new roles, or even demoted or fired. The larger the organisation the larger the change programme you will find. If may be a formal transformation programme, or it may just be a collection of smaller changes spanning the organisation.

Change is always made for good business reasons at the time, and with the best intentions of those leading the change. There will be an objective regarding the future of the business and goals set that have to be achieved. Much work will be done looking at future sales, markets, competition, organisational performance, budgets, resources, operating models, functions, staffing levels, resource levels, roles, etc., etc. All of these are the nuts and bolts of the business, and the organisational design puts it all together to achieve a desired end state. There is only one thing missing, one thing hardly ever considered – the emotional engagement of the people that will either make it work or not. Winning their hearts and minds. This is not simply communication, people management, or a token gesture towards keeping staff on-side to be seen to be doing the right thing, it is an authentic and genuine care for the impact on people, and delivered with complete integrity.

> *"Clients do not come first. Employees come first."*
> – Richard Branson

The people that make a business what it is are not 'Human Resources'. Resources suggest a business asset to be utilised (which is how many see them), and 'Human' is just a depersonalised term to refer to the fact they are living breathing human beings. The people that walk through the office door every morning are husbands, wives, sons, daughters, fathers, mothers, friends, carers, and so on. They have ambitions, fears, worries, stresses, beliefs, and values. They have ups and downs, good days and bad. They are all unique and how they respond to change is what makes the difference to any business. The best plans and models will be extremely painful and costly to deliver without the support of the people that will make it a reality. In practice people are pushed, cajoled, bribed, and otherwise encouraged and forced into the organisational structure and new roles. If they don't fit, then ultimately, they are pushed out. They are simply expected to 'get on board' with the changes.

Every change has an effect on the most important component – the people that run the business. From boardroom to shop floor everyone one is potentially impacted by even the most modest of changes. How they respond has very little to do with their role, skillset, or career path. It has everything to do with who they are as a person, what else is going on in their lives at that time, and what they value. By making sure every individual is understood and supported through the change with empathy and integrity, many if not all can be kept completely engaged – the critical difference between success and failure. This should not be dismissed as being 'soft' or unnecessary, this should be encouraged as enlightened leadership. Emotional intelligence is widely reported as a critical leadership skill for the 21st century.

Most leaders will say their staff are their most precious resource. A time of change, unsettling for most people, is the time to demonstrate this. In this book I will show you why this is so critical, and how to make change, even when many people are adversely impacted, with compassion, integrity, and with the maximum engagement of your people.

CEOs and executive teams are constantly under pressure and are expected to exert clear and decisive leadership. They are expected to have the answers, know where the company is going, and how to get there. They are not expected to be unsure, or have doubts, or ask for input or help. i.e. the typical executive leadership environment is not conducive to emotional intelligent behaviours. This can quickly become part of the culture and the behaviour replicated down through all layers of management. Taking time to listen to people, hear their concerns and ideas, and being prepared to compromise or even change plans (but still achieve the objective) is not a sign of weakness, it is actually a strength and requires a confident leader. If this behaviour becomes part of the company culture, then then emotional intelligence will grow throughout the organisation.

The benefits of making change with emotional intelligence and with the full engagement of staff are huge and will last for many years. It is not just the initial cost savings that come from saved management time, maintaining productivity, avoided recruitment costs for replacing staff, and possibly avoided legal and settlement costs. There is also a huge amount of time saved in implementing the change. But the real benefits come with maintaining morale, motivation, trust, respect, and loyalty of staff. The value of which is priceless and will be felt for many years to come. Beyond this there is the reputational benefits that will reach far and wide within and beyond the boundaries of the business.

"In life, change is inevitable,
in business change is vital."
– Warren G. Bennis

Organisational Changes

It is not just large-scale changes like a merger, acquisition,
or reorganisation. It is also everyday minor changes such
as a change in reporting lines, appraisals, pay reviews,
recruitment of a new team member, and so on, that can have
a profound impact on individuals and should be handled
with care. Ironically, it is usually the junior manager, the
least experienced layer of management, that is executing
the change and having the difficult conversations.

There are many different reasons why organisations change and the scale of change can vary enormously. Some changes can seem innocuous but often have implications and consequences that could have been avoided with anticipation and careful handling. Some are seemingly very minor, and others have massive impacts. Consider the following scenarios amongst others.

Promotion

Good news for all involved, right? What could go wrong? Certainly, for the individual involved this is good news and usually accompanied by a welcome pay rise and a big announcement. The individual is congratulated and given worthy recognition. This single event will undoubtedly cause every other member of their team to consider their own position. Some will be perfectly happy for the individual involved, but some will not be. Why weren't they considered for promotion? How long until they will be? Some may feel overlooked. Relationships will be affected – perhaps the promoted individual is now in a more senior position and has increased authority. The dynamics of the team are changed. Even when the promotion made is fully justified the ripples of the change can cause some to feel unsettled and uncomfortable.

It would be easy to dismiss such consequences as irrational or simply not relevant. However, the line manager still needs the skills to handle the situation and achieve a quick and positive outcome. Otherwise, a minor disgruntlement can become a constant sore point and grow into a bigger issue over time. Even the most modest of changes, seemingly completely positive, need to be handled with care.

Reporting Lines

Perhaps the change does not involve anyone moving up or down the organisation and is just a sideways move. This will involve a change of reporting lines for one or more members of staff. It is widely recognised that the relationship between the individual and his or her line manager is the single most important factor in their job satisfaction. A simple sideways move or change of reporting lines can be a major boost to someone's career, but it can also have devastating consequences for others.

If the relationship works well and the line manager has good leadership skills and emotional intelligence the individual will flourish. If the relationship is strained, the line manager blinkered by poor skills or ignorance, then the individual will suffer and so will their performance. Either way the responsibility for the relationship is shared between the individual and the line manager. If the line manager looks no further than the authority of his or her role to make the change then relationship will flounder. As with any form of relationship, it requires investment by both parties to make it work.

Recruitment

A new recruit to a team will change the dynamics. This could be for better or worse, but they will change. The new team member may bring many new skills and talents, or not. They may also build strong professional relationships or they may ruffle many feathers, i.e. the square peg in a round hole scenario. Many highly skilled and respected individuals have been recruited into a role and failed spectacularly. This is not through any fault of their own (they were recruited for their skills and experience, and went all the way through the recruitment process). Any new individual introduced into a team and organisation will have an impact – good, bad, or indifferent. Some existing staff may have applied for the role and have been unsuccessful, others may feel threatened by the skills of new recruit (possibly including the line manager). From establishing a new working relationship with the recruit, to helping him or her bond with the team, and managing the impacts on other staff, the line manager needs to manage each relationship with skill and emotional intelligence.

Losing Staff

Even in the most stable of organisations staff will leave from time to time. It may be voluntary, or not. The circumstances may be positive and celebrated, e.g. retirement of respected colleague, or totally negative (redundancy or termination of employment). Not only will this leave a gap to be filled and have implications on workload, but more importantly the circumstance will affect those that remain. Someone fired from their role or simply made redundant will cause a high level of insecurity in some, if not all, remaining staff. The ability to manage this change, and how it is received by others, needs skill, understanding, and empathy. Even if the loss of a team member is for positive reasons this will have consequences on the rest of the team. Will the person be replaced? Will they be expected to absorb extra workload? Is there a vacancy to be applied for? Whatever the outcome the team dynamics are changed.

Reorganisation

Many organisations will make regular structural changes to support the changing demands on the business. This will involve one or more of the above scenarios with all of the consequences described.

This means that most if not all of the management teams at all levels will be involved. Coordination will be put in place and possibly someone allocated to manage the transition. Inevitably it is the line manager that has to manage the communication and difficult discussions with individuals and teams. By definition these are usually junior managers with the least staff management experience. The most critical element of managing and implementing change is therefore in the hands of those with the least experience, and usually without the relevant training and support to guide them through it!

Mergers & Acquisitions

Beyond changes within the organisation we have changes in a broader context affecting the future of the organisation as a whole. This affects the individual not just in the ways described above but brings many other additional questions in to consideration:

- Culture – whether it is a merger, acquisition, or sale, the resulting organisation will have a different culture. This will affect every member of staff, and by implication every customer.

- Location – This level of change often raises questions for some, if not all, staff regarding future location, relocation issues, and implications for working hours or home-working arrangements.

- Roles & Functions – almost inevitably for some staff their roles will change, and the function they are part of will change. In extreme cases it will be removed or relocated leaving them completely vulnerable.

- Pay Grades, Pensions, Benefits – all can be subject to review and change. Inevitably in a merger or acquisition there are differences and often these need to be reconciled meaning change for some.

- Career Path – the change may increase or diminish the value of the individual's chosen career path. Perhaps a long-term future with the organisation is now more attractive, or less so.

Process Improvement

Some changes are not structural. For example, a process improvement initiative designed to increase efficiencies and reduce costs. The objective is sound and easily understood, but changing processes means changing someone's job – perhaps several roles. Many will welcome changes that make the job easier, others will be sceptical or cynical about the changes, and some will simply feel threatened by the unknown. It is human nature to find comfort in habits and known processes – taking this away from those that 'have always done it this way', even for the right reasons, can be very disruptive.

Cultural Changes

Similarly, any initiative to simply change the culture within an organisation may not involve any structural changes. It may be a well-intended initiative to rejuvenate the organisation's vision, mission statement, and values. If this is successful, and sponsored from the top, it will be expected to permeate every corner of the organisation, and all staff will be expected to engage with it. Some will be positive and buy-in to the changes or at least see the career enhancing benefits! Others will be resistant, sceptical, and dismissive.

Leadership Changes

The trigger for many organisational changes is often a result of change within the leadership team. Particularly at senior levels leaders have their own strong preferences, based on their personal experience, of how they like to operate, and what they expect from their teams. In addition, they will often recruit former colleagues where they already have a proven working relationship – often overlooking existing internal candidates in the process.

Apart from the direct implications of such changes, most staff in the organisation will know that a new recruit in the leadership team will inevitably lead to change. Some will go out of their way to sound out the new recruit and make good first impressions, and others will tread very cautiously and with suspicion. Either way, a new recruit at senior levels will be expected to make changes, and the simple fact that there is a new recruit at this level will mean many new relationships will need to be established. For some this will mean managing 'upwards' and establishing a relationship with a new manager, or perhaps a new peer. Whatever the specific nuances of the relationship, to simply manage it on a purely business or professional level only misses an opportunity to establish a stronger more successful relationship.

Pay Reviews

Probably the most sensitive, and certainly one of the most valuable aspects of our relationship with our employer. If we are fortunate, we get many things from our job – satisfaction of overcoming intellectual, creative, and physical challenges, recognition of our performance and contribution, and the camaraderie of being part of a bigger team. But ultimately, we work to live and our pay, particularly for the main breadwinners, is what supports our families and enables the lives that we lead.

Those who are involved in determining and delivering pay reviews will know it is a minefield of expectations, performance ratings, and budget constraints. Even the most experienced manager will be challenged by mismatched expectations – often from their most valuable staff (because they know it). Managing this change to the pay of their team members, while keeping them fully engaged, needs understanding, empathy, and the ability to manage the employee/employer relationship at its most critical point.

Appraisals & Staff Issues

Similarly, annual appraisals, normally conducted by direct line managers, are personal conversations that go to the heart of the staff/line manager relationship – the thing that has the greatest impact on the morale and job satisfaction of the individual involved.

Every organisation has its process, which normally involves evaluation of an employee's performance against a written job description. It is an essential part of any staff management process and an opportunity to gauge performance against stated objectives and deliverables – obviously some will struggle to meet the required standard, others will meet it, and some will outperform. A prepared line manager will usually have evidence and keep the discussion as objective as possible.

The appraisal discussion itself should be a two-way conversation, allowing the individual the opportunity to assess their own performance against their understanding of the role. The line manager and individual are reviewing the same thing but from different perspectives. If there is a strong relationship in place, and 'no surprises' during the conversation, then there will be close agreement on the outcome. However even in this case there may still be a difference of views in specific areas. This may well be considered as a change in understanding or expectation by the individual.

Similarly, this process makes no provision for the fact that every individual is unique and a complex mixture of skills, talents, experiences, personality, genetics, upbringing, culture, family, and current circumstances, to name just a few factors. Even the most thorough of job descriptions is only a crude definition of what is expected of the individual, and as perceived by the line manager. Recognising the individual as a person, with much to offer, and evaluating performance in one specific role, requires emotional intelligence that is often not sufficiently developed in the line manager – simply because of lack of experience. There are examples of the 'square peg in a round hole' in any organisation. To dismiss such an individual (in both meanings of the word) can be missing an opportunity to use the same resource to great effect, as well as being unjust.

Growing Pains

Another example of change that is not a direct result of structural reorganisation, is the growing pains that successful businesses go through during periods of rapid growth. A small business, where everybody knows everybody and things are done through common understanding, will often struggle when that is no longer the case and formal controls and processes are needed. Individuals need to adapt, often frequently, and new working practices can often become outdated and need replacing.

> *"When we change our thinking, we change our lives."*
> – Stephen R. Covey

As we can see change takes many forms, and whatever the reason or type of change in a business or organisation, it will affect one or more people – and quite often the entire organisation. Addressing only the mechanics of the change – roles, functions, reporting lines, workflow, operating models, and so on, may be an essential but to only focus on this misses the single most critical element: the people that will make it happen.

People are a fluid mixture of hopes, dreams, emotions, anxieties, and worries, they have good days and bad, they have strong relationships, and poor ones. They have values, morals, beliefs, faiths, and cultural influences. They are at different stages of their lives and careers, and have differing priorities. They cannot be put pigeon-holed or treated as widget that is part of a machine. Only by putting the same level of care and attention on the people that make the business tick can any form of change be made effectively – otherwise it becomes painful, slow, and costly.

Exercise

Your organisation is not in a static state, and you will be facing changes, probably in multiple areas. These may relate to your specific role, your team, or your whole business. It may be the changes are driven by external influences such as market forces, political, or regulatory controls. Make a note of all the changes that you are facing today:

"Failure isn't fatal,
but failure to change might be."
– John Wooden

The Challenges

Organisational change is never easy and takes a lot of time
and effort. Planning and design of change is of little value
if poorly executed. The key to success is the engagement of
staff and the astute leadership of the senior team to do so.

As we have seen, change is constant, both in the business world and our personal lives. All changes affect one or more individuals – the people in our business, the people that <u>are</u> our business. When planning a small-scale change or large-scale transformation programme within a business there are several challenges to be addressed:

Objective and Goals

The first challenge is to be clear on the end state – what is the change designed to achieve and how will you know? Once this has been established, how will you obtain the buy-in of all employees so they engage and commit to it? Some will say that this is irrelevant and that the objectives and goals will be set down by the 'leadership' team and everyone will be expected to 'get on board'. As we will see, this is one way of doing it, but without an engaged and motivated workforce it will be unnecessarily painful and slow.

Time and Effort

Next the change needs to be planned and it will take time and effort, often from the most valuable resources, to implement. This additional workload on the organisation will put more pressure on teams and resources as they continue to do their day-to-day job. During a period of change many staff are simply expected to absorb the extra workload and juggle this with the existing commitments.

If staff are motivated by the change and have bought in to reasons for it and the benefits it will bring, then the motivation will be there. However, without this they will struggle to understand why they should absorb the extra workload, and struggle to make allowances for it.

Budgets

A formal change project will take time and will usually involve other explicit costs such as external consultants, interim staff, etc. This can be quantified against explicit plans at the outset, but what cannot be quantified are the indirect costs and consequential costs of the change. A drop in productivity, a delay to customer projects, recruitment fees for replacing staff, management time to cover staff issues, and so on. All of these represent a risk to the project budget, but that risk can be mitigated with the engagement and commitment of all staff.

Difficult Discussions

Many changes will have potentially negative impacts on some staff – it may be an individual, or it may be the entire organisation, and there will be difficult discussions to be had. A successful discussion will include mutual understanding of positions as well as the goal of the conversation. If it proceeds well a way forward will be agreed, no matter how unpalatable. To achieve this result, the discussion will often be kept objective and business-like, and in many cases, that will be sufficient. However, in others, where the emotions of the individual are sparked, then careful handling by the line manager, with emotional intelligence, will be determine how successful or not the discussions are.

If the discussion is handled effectively, then even where there is significant impact to the individual, an understanding can be maintained, as well as the trust and respect of the participants. If it goes badly, then the issues and challenges can be magnified, extend to involve the wider management team, run on for several months, and possibly end up with legal and financial implications.

Keeping Customer Focus

Another challenge when making change, of any size, is keeping staff focused on their role – delivering products and services to their customers. Change creates uncertainty, and uncertainty is unsettling. While there will always be unanswered questions during a period of change, by keeping staff engaged during this period it is possible to keep them focused on their role. If they feel disengaged, and threatened by the change, then their personal priorities will lie elsewhere. The resultant lack of focus on their role and the customer will ultimately damage the business. Again, all of this can be avoided, or at least minimised, by managing the change with understanding and empathy, i.e. with the use of emotional intelligence.

Staff Engagement

Every change is disruptive and unsettling – it is human nature. With every organisational change, no matter how large or small, the change needs to be made with the full engagement of staff to avoid any of the negative consequences. But this will not happen by default. Assuming that staff will remain fully engaged is an unnecessary risk to take.

Clients & Suppliers

If the change is significant then news of the changes will reach clients and suppliers. Whilst both will understand that this is an internal matter and should be transparent to them, in practice some will have good and established working relationships with staff members and any disruption will become a concern to them. Suppliers in particular will be wary of changes to the leadership team that may lead to changes to budgets or priorities. Clients will be concerned about the organisation's direction and long-term plans. Either way, the implications of change within a business can reach beyond its boundaries, and the impacts to relationships at an individual personal level need to be considered.

Change Management

All of the above are recognised challenges for any change project. Formal change management methodology will guide the organisation through the discrete phases of the project. There are many well established models such as the McKinsey Change Management Framework, or Kotter's Change Management Model. They all include detailed analysis of the current state, design of the new state to be achieved, and all of the components involved such as functions, roles, and staff mapping. They also address the 'soft' or people side of change in terms of communication and involving staff. It is understood that that there will be resistance from the people impacted, and that this needs to be overcome. But how? This is what the remainder of this book addresses.

There are practical steps that can be put in place such as training, support networks, and one-to-one coaching, and all are aimed at winning the hearts and minds of the individual, i.e. getting them each personally to a point in their personal change curve where they can commit. Overcoming the resistance to change is the pivotal moment in any change programme. Let us look at change resistance in more detail.

*"Procrastination is another
form of resistance."*
– Louise Hay

The Resistance

*Very rarely will an individual or a team be explicit and
vocal in their concerns and issues about change. It is
sponsored from the top and it is counter-intuitive to do so.
However, their reluctance will manifest itself in other ways.*

Reasons for Resistance

There are many reasons why an individual may resist change. It is a personal perspective and often different between individuals in the same team. Consider occasions when you have not yet reached the point of accepting a change. It probably included one or more of the following reasons. This is not an exhaustive list:

- Threat to individual authority
- Threat to the value or power of the team
- Negative impact to salary or earning potential
- Impact to image or reputation
- Loss of expected opportunities
- Threat to job security
- Reduction in team budgets or resources
- Lack of clarity on processes
- Mistrust of leadership
- Additional workload during the period of change
- Additional workload following the change
- Not sold on the 'why', i.e. the need to change
- Threat to existing relationships – colleagues, customers, and suppliers
- Lack of information about the change – real or perceived

When an individual is resisting change, they will have their own reasons – conscious and subconscious – which will probably include some of the above. This can and does lead to negative thinking and they will search out other reasons to justify their view, and seek the input of others to validate it.

Symptoms of Resistance

Vary rarely will an individual be explicit and direct in their resistance to change. Most will realise this would be a career limiting move when the change has been led from above! Anyone who is clear and vocal in their resistance is either very confident in their position because they know they can secure a new job with ease, or they no longer care and are already looking for their next job. For everyone else tact and diplomacy is required to raise their concerns without jeopardising their position. There are several symptoms to resistance to change within an organisation including the following:

- Drop in productivity
  A general drop in productivity is a culmination of small acts of procrastination. Emails take longer to get a response, tasks that could be completed today are allowed to slip to tomorrow. Breaks stretch out longer and people are more inclined to leave the office on time.

- Rumour and gossip
  Even if you do not detect the rumours and gossip directly, you can observe the increase chat in the kitchens and corridors. A trusted advisor will always share the office gossip and what people are really saying about the change.

- Lost hours
  This can be anything from increased sick leave and absenteeism, to simply staff not arriving early or staying late. Tea and lunch breaks can become extended and once productive time is now lost.

- Morale
  Empathy with others, and self-awareness, of feelings and moods will detect any change in morale. The facial expressions, body language, and general demeanour of staff will all be indicators of morale within the team.

- Slow Decisions
  Decisions will take longer to reach and decisions that staff were once comfortable to make themselves will now be deferred or passed upwards. This is not a direct act of resistance but a reflection that the individual is less prepared to put the thought and effort in to making the decision and acting on it.

- Reluctance to take on new tasks
  Similarly, an agreement to take on new assignments will be met with increased reluctance. In a period of insecurity, with current workloads taking longer to deliver, staff will be less inclined to take on new work.

This is not an exhaustive list; resistance can manifest itself in many ways. The manager and leadership must use their own emotional intelligence, and own self-awareness of relationships and morale, to determine if staff are resisting change, or whether they are fully engaged and supportive. In which case all of the symptoms above will provide positive indications.

Overcoming Resistance

In the following chapters we will look at how change can be managed to overcome resistance, and possibly avoid it in the first place. But first, let us look at why it is so important and valuable to do so.

*"Everything we do
has consequences."*
– Dennis Potter

Consequences

*Change is unsettling at the best of times. A large-scale
change in the workplace can be traumatic for some. A drop
in morale, loss of valuable people, resistance to change,
management overhead, and impacts to productivity
can be mitigated, if not avoided all together.*

The consequences of not managing change effectively, by simply imposing it without emotional intelligence, are all too common. Typically, this will include some, if not all, of the following.

Morale

Usually the first thing to suffer across teams, if not the whole organisation. Uncertainty and lack of information will breed worry and have staff reaching to update their CV. The drop in morale will be palpable and will dominate conversation. The hearts and minds of staff will not be on day to day operations and making the business a success, it will be on their own personal situation. Even the most positive and constructive of people will feel the effects of a drop in morale of the people around them.

Morale is not only impacted by negative changes, even positive changes like acquisition of a new business, expansion in to a new geography, or building new products and services, can have implications. Some may feel very uncertain about the change and what it means for their role, and others may feel threatened by the change. Everyone will consider what it means to them personally. Some will see it as good news and positive, others will be unsure and full of questions, and others will know their role will change and not welcome it.

This does not only apply to organisation-wide changes, even a change for one individual will have implications for their wider team. Negativity will breed negativity and soon a change for one person can become a much wider issue, and impact team morale. Low team morale can spread so the direct impact to one individual can ripple out across many areas of the business.

Productivity

As a result of a dip in morale, productivity will fall, not just as a result of a lack of focus, but also a reluctance to put in the extra time and effort that may be required. Staff may become disengaged – they may fulfil their role and their hours but simply 'work to rule' and not be prepared to go the extra mile. Others may take it further and prioritise job-hunting over doing the one they have got.

The indirect impacts of a drop in productivity are significant: higher costs, drop in customer service, and missed deadlines.

Valued Staff are Lost

Good people know their value and know how much demand there is for their skills. These are the ones that find it easiest to walk into a new role and a period of change, if not handled correctly, can see the best staff leaving for pastures new. Conversely, those staff that do not command the best of reputations or have been marginalised also know it. They will cling to their role in the hope of not being impacted. So a period of change can result in the worst of both worlds – the best staff leaving, and those that are less critical doing their very best to stay.

The critical point here, the point of no return, is to avoid valued staff even considering other options. No matter how the organisational change may unfold, once a person has updated his or her CV and started to look at other options, he or she will nearly always find something that looks more appealing. They are 'lost' to the organisation once they are motivated to look outside it, so managing change effectively, to not give them this motivation is essential.

Trust Eroded

Depending on how the change is managed, trust can very easily be eroded. A period of change, and the uncertainty that comes with it, brings heightened senses. People become tuned in to body language, tone of voice, off-the-cuff remarks, regardless of what is actually said. They will observe who is meeting with whom, who is chatting over lunch or outside the office, and with the use of shared calendars they will be tracking every meeting and appointment, to try and make sense of gossip and rumour. People will very quickly feel they are not being informed and are kept in the dark – even when this is not the case. The perception will become their reality. Avoiding this is not just about communication, it is also about understanding the concern of the individual and managing them with empathy, honesty, and integrity.

Customer Service

Inevitably customer service will be impacted. Even if not a conscious decision by staff, the drop in morale, the distraction of change, and the lack of focus will eventually become apparent to customers.

Where strong personal relationships exist between a staff member and a customer (or supplier), confidential information might be shared and knowledge of the changes will be leaked to the outside world. This in turn will give cause for concern to customers (and suppliers).

Projects Delayed

Similarly, the impact to productivity will hit any projects that are in progress. Not only will schedules be compromised, but the staff engaged and responsible, will be less inclined to take corrective action. Ultimately this too will impact customers. It may be a customer facing project that is delayed, or an internal project to deliver improvements or efficiencies to the organisation – ultimately the customer is adversely affected.

Reputation

All of these consequences can ultimately affect the reputation of a business – in the eyes of customers that may perceive a drop in service, as an employer among the current workforce and industry in general, and even in the eyes of suppliers. The impact may be short-lived, or not, but damage to a reputation takes a lot more time and effort to repair than it does to avoid in the first place.

In many cases, a poorly managed change will incur all the consequences listed above. Even when a change only directly applies to one individual the ripple effect can spread across an entire organisation. For example, an employee that is considered to be unfairly treated (whether he or she is or not) and dismissed, can send shockwaves throughout the organisation. This could easily lead to all of the consequences outlined above, but could also be easily avoided.

Applying Emotional Intelligence, and managing the change with care, is by no means a guarantee that these issues can be avoided, but they can be greatly mitigated and reduced. This in turn can reduce, if not eliminate, a lot of the pain to individuals and organisations that can go with instigating and applying change.

*"Great things in business are never done by one person,
they are done by a team of people"*
– Steve Jobs

The Prize – Getting It Right

*Keep staff engaged and motivated, and productivity and
morale can be maintained. Huge amounts of management
time can be saved, and key people retained. Recruitment costs
and customer impacts can be avoided. The loyalty and respect
that can be generated by a well-managed change is priceless.*

Before we look at what Emotional Intelligence is, and how we can apply it in the business context, consider the benefits of getting it right.

It is not simply a matter of avoiding the negative consequences – although this is a significant reason in its own right. Avoiding the impact to morale, and therefore motivation and productivity is an obvious benefit. Keeping staff engaged and focused on their roles is critical to the business. Maintaining customer service and project schedules also maintains reputation and confidence in employees, customers, and suppliers.

On top of this, managing change with care for all those involved brings additional benefits:

Integrity

When staff can see that a difficult decision has been made with great care and understanding, and that it has been addressed with genuine empathy and support for all those affected it can actually increase respect and loyalty from employees – because that is what they see being given to their colleagues. Not only does it avoid the negative consequences it actually reinforces the trust and mutual respect between staff, their managers, and the leadership of the business.

This is true generically, but is never more crucial than in the specific and direct relationship between and individual and his or her line manager. A poorly handled conversation can damage the relationship, result in a loss of trust and respect, and fail to resolve the issue or agree a way forward.

Conversely, if the same conversation had been handled with genuine care and empathy, then respect and trust can be maintained, and the relationship strengthened. A difficult conversation may still be had, and the issue may not be resolved, but integrity has been upheld and the conversation can continue constructively.

Innovation

More often than not employees, as they have direct hands-on experience of the issues and challenges being faced, and therefore a different perspective, will have good and novel ideas that may not have been considered. These may or may not have value and adopted, but simply allowing staff the opportunity to contribute in itself will be seen as positive, and build trust. They will feel that they are being listened to and have had the opportunity to contribute.

The simple act of listening to (really listening to, not simply hearing) employees demonstrates empathy. Their input needs to be sought, and handled with respect even if it is not implemented. However, in many cases they will provide valuable insight and good ideas worthy of consideration.

Time and Effort

A smoothly implemented change by definition will not take as long or require as much effort. This is not just for all those that are involved, but it also saves significant management time in dealing with the negative consequences and fall out of change.

Any staff issue, particularly if it involves a formal grievance or dispute can be extremely costly both in management time, and in financial terms. By avoiding or at least minimising this impact managers and business leaders have a much higher capacity to focus on the things that really matter.

Bottom Line

Ultimately the reward for managing change effectively will be a boost to the bottom line. A huge amount of money can be saved by avoiding additional recruitment fees (as well as tribunal costs and compromise agreements), and by saving the time and effort spent on implementing the changes. Maintaining morale and productivity can be tied directly to maintaining and growing revenues.

Loyalty

There are longer lasting and more deeply rooted advantages in managing change with care. Even if the change is difficult and have negative impacts, if staff are engaged, with the leadership, and feel they are on the same side, then loyalty can increase significantly – but this only happens when it is clearly two-way.

Loyalty is not only between the individual and their employer, and vice versa, it is between the individual and their direct leadership – it is very personal. This loyalty or lack of loyalty, can therefore be a significant factor in the careers of all involved long after this particular change has been and gone.

Reputation

Similarly, for the same reasons, the reputation of an employer and the individuals involved in leading the change, can be enhanced or diminished by how well or not the change is managed. With the advent of social media and information sharing instantaneously, reputations can spread far and wide, and comments posted on the internet exist for eternity.

Overcoming resistance

There are several ways that resistance can be reduced or overcome. Some are practical such as breaking the change down in to smaller, more palatable steps. Or perhaps putting additional resources in place to help with the transition, allowing more time for changes to be implemented, and so on.

However, at the heart of resistance are the people, and effective strategies for overcoming resistance always come back to effective engagement of people, by the leadership team. This includes clear communication, giving opportunities for staff to contribute, listening to feedback, utilising the skills and strengths of individuals, and so on. But the onus is also on the leader to show flexibility, passion, motivation, and to remain positive and constructive. In short, a high level of emotional intelligence is required to avoid or overcome resistance to change, and this is critical to the success of the change programme.

It is still widely reported that 60–70% of change initiatives will fail. The reasons are varied and complex but not managing the people and personal elements of change is the greatest risk. Ensuring leaders have the appropriate skills, and do not simply pass off change management to others, is an essential element of successfully managing change.

Part 2:
Emotional Intelligence

"It is true that integrity alone will not make you a leader, but without integrity you will never be one."
— Zig Ziglar

Emotional Intelligence

Why is it that the most intelligent people sometimes make poor leaders? Why is it that others less well qualified can inspire and lead with ease? Emotional Intelligence is the difference that makes a difference.

What is Emotional Intelligence (EI) and why does it matter?

A typical definition is as follows:

> Emotional Intelligence: (noun) *the capacity to be aware of, control, and express one's emotions, and to handle interpersonal relationships judiciously and empathetically.*

If we unpack the definition, we see the need for self-awareness – not just to understand our own emotions and their causes, but also to control them. We also see the need to understand the emotions of others, and their causes, i.e. empathy, and to handle them with care.

From a theoretical perspective there are actually a number of different models used to define Emotional Intelligence. Although the term was first used in the 1960s, the common understanding was popularised by the American psychologist Daniel Goleman in the 1990s.

He identified five key elements to Emotional Intelligence:

- Self-awareness
- Self-control
- Motivation
- Empathy
- Social skills

To be self-aware means to understand your emotions, what influences them, how these emotions, and your resulting behaviours affect others. It also means you understand your character and personality, you understand your strengths and weaknesses, and you are able to demonstrate humility.

Self-control means you are able to regulate your emotions and responses. You will understand when you are losing control and be able to change the situation. You will respond to others objectively and not respond to provocation. You will also hold yourself to account for your emotions and responses to others – you will know when you have behaved correctly, or allowed your emotions to cloud your judgement.

Motivation in this context is striving to maintain the standards you have set yourself, the way you want to behave, and how you want to treat others. It is usually accompanied by optimism and a constructive attitude to find a solution and way forward whatever the circumstances. There is a desire to do the right thing by the individual, as well as the employer, and anyone else that may be involved.

To demonstrate empathy, you need to be able to put yourself in someone else's position and see things from their perspective. This is not to see things from their perspective through the lens of your own agenda and objectives, but to genuinely understand their position. You will be able to interpret all the signs of communication – body language, tone of voice, silences, as well as what they say, and be a good judge of their feelings and emotions.

The social skills element of Emotional Intelligence means you are able to adapt and respond to a wide variety of situations with the same levels of understanding and empathy. You can handle bad news and difficult situations as well as good news and easy discussions. You are good at conflict resolution, bring parties together, and find a way forward that maintains respect of all involved.

All of this means that in the business context a dialogue is not purely a functional business conversation. It is not just about exchanging information. There is a personal and emotional connection. Whilst there are rare situations where a discussion should be kept at a purely business level, in nearly all cases applying emotional intelligence, and displaying empathy, will bring many benefits. Empathy demonstrates understanding and should not be confused with agreement or compromise – it costs nothing to act with empathy.

Emotional intelligence and its use in business is not new. The 1998 *Harvard Business Review* paper 'What Makes a Great Leader' states that: "The most effective leaders are all alike in one crucial way, they all have a high degree of ... emotional intelligence."

In 2011 a study of recruiting managers found that 71% stated they valued EI (Emotional Intelligence) over IQ. This was for several reasons including:

- High EI employees are better at staying calm under pressure
- They listen as often, or more often, than they speak
- They lead by example
- They make more thoughtful business decisions

But what is becoming more widely understood is just how critical this is to the success of a business. Entrepreneur Gary Vaynerchuck recently stated that "We are on the dawn of an era where Emotional Intelligence is about to become the single most important skill."

The following chapters will look at what it means to be emotionally intelligent, what traits and behaviours someone with high EI will demonstrate, and how to apply these in the business context. But first let us look at why this is so critical.

We have seen that businesses are constantly changing, and that this change affects the people in our businesses – it is they who have to adapt and adopt the change, and they who will determine if it is applied effectively and with ease, or is resisted and becomes a massive challenge to the business with serious negative consequences. It is the people – not the roles, not the job titles, but the people who are emotional beings who make decisions and take actions for emotional reasons.

When people are not emotionally engaged, and do not make the personal commitment to engage with change, then conscious and subconscious resistance usually follows. There is often a tangible drop in morale, and then productivity. People become less inclined to put extra effort in so deadlines are missed and projects delayed. Decisions get deferred and processes take longer to complete. The cost to an organisation of people that are not engaged and supportive of change is huge. The increase in management time alone is significant.

By applying emotional intelligence to our interactions, whether it is communicating a major reorganisation, discussing an annual appraisal, or just making introductions, we can have a much more effective and constructive dialogue. We can ensure people are engaged in the change process, and help them get to the point of personal commitment and support for the change sooner.

"It is very important to understand that emotional intelligence is not the opposite of intelligence, it is not the triumph of heart over head, it is the unique intersection of both."
– David Caruso

12 EI Traits and Behaviours

You cannot acquire emotional intelligence by studying, you have to practice it and learn from your behaviours and the responses it generates from others and from within yourself. You have to question your emotions and the emotions of others, and ask why? You have to be open to the perspective of others, and you have to be open to learning about yourself.

The following section describes the common traits and behaviours of someone with high emotional intelligence. Like any intelligence they can be developed, and some may be stronger than others, or come more naturally than others. They can be identified, or not, in other people and can be an indicator of the level of emotional intelligence that exists in a relationship. The behaviours that accompany emotional intelligence can be practised and become habit. As you read through the list identify the ones that you need to practice.

These traits and behaviours are not a compromise on 'academic' intelligence and understanding, they do not come at a 'cost' of sacrificing current beliefs. They are an added and new perspective on relationships (any relationship, in this context with staff, superiors, customers, suppliers, etc.). They are an enhancement, an additional layer of intelligence.

The following are traits and behaviours of someone with high emotional intelligence:

1. You think about feelings – yours and others
    From the definition of emotional intelligence, you are aware of your own feelings, and those of others. You understand that people's behaviour is largely driven by their feelings. You take time to think about feelings, where they came from, the reasons behind them, whether they are valid and appropriate or perhaps misplaced. You are not scared to examine your own feelings and the cause of them.

2. You take time to think
    When facing a situation or discussion, or perhaps in the middle of it, you avoid knee-jerk reactions and losing

control. You take time to pause, breathe, think and respond calmly. You do not rush to react.

3. You think about your thinking
   Similarly, you think about your thinking. Is it constructive? Is it positive? Is it logical? It is quite possible to separate your emotions from your thinking, but if your thinking is negative, then you may need to change the way you think about things. Emotionally intelligent people are aware of how they are thinking and are able to change it if need be.

4. You learn about yourself
   You question your responses and reactions. You also look at the consequences of your actions and any feedback you have received. You may not like it, but you are able to separate your emotional response from a rational assessment of how you have acted.

5. You are authentic
   You are comfortable with who you are, you are happy with your values and beliefs, and you act accordingly. You do not pretend to be something you are not, or act in a way that is contrary to your values just because someone else may expect it or demand it.

6. You demonstrate empathy
   You can reflect back to an individual that you understand their views and feelings. This does not mean you have to agree with them, but you understand them, and can show that you understand them.

7. You demonstrate humility
   Often lacking by leaders in the business context as they

see it as a sign of weakness, but to act with integrity and authenticity means you are able to demonstrate humility when it is right to do so. Not everyone has all the answers or is right about everything all the time. An empathetic leader will listen as much, if not more, than they talk.

8. You give praise and feedback
   You can give positive and constructive feedback, as well as negative. You understand the importance of this to the individual and positive effect it can have. It becomes easy and important to you to give praise where it is due.

9. You apologise, and forgive
   You are able to apologise where necessary, and are able to forgive others where need be. You can be gracious when you are wrong, and have been wronged. This is not the same as accepting repeated failures and not a sign of weakness. It is a strength to be able to act with integrity and do the right thing.

10. You reject politics and egos
    If you are acting with emotional intelligence, and with authenticity, then you recognise when others do not exhibit the same behaviour, and it feels in conflict with your values. When others are acting out of personal advantage you do not become entangled or involved.

11. You are open to change
    By understanding your reactions, your thoughts and emotions, and that of others, you become open and more accepting of change.

12. You look forward, not back
    Similarly, emotionally intelligent people tend to be

more positive and constructive. As such they are more likely to look forward and to look for solutions, and learn from the past, rather than clinging to the past and bemoaning the changes.

Many of the above traits show that emotionally intelligent people are self-aware. As with all of the above it can take a long period of self-discovery and questioning and examining to reach this level of understanding. But it is not just self-awareness that is important, with this needs to be self-acceptance to behave with authenticity and integrity.

CASE STUDY

The examples below are from real life situations, but the names have been changed to protect the innocent as well as the guilty!

New Manager – How not to do it

Martin was appointed the manager of a team of senior and experienced resources. The team were hard working and generally performed well, but there were some issues with certain company processes not always being followed correctly.

Martin wanted to establish himself as the manager of the team and called an off-site team meeting. The meeting started well and Martin started to emphasise the importance of the company processes being followed. The team could not argue with his logic and sat in silence. Not sure that the message had fully landed he stressed the point again and again, and as his frustration rose, he used stronger and stronger language to ram the point home. The team were now feeling uncomfortable, they understood the point, but were dismayed at the behaviour of their new manager. Still not getting the response he expected, ultimately Martin started getting quite emotional and threatened that anyone who did not comply would be disciplined.

Finally, the painful meeting ended. The team understood the points that were made, but were disappointed at the way there were treated, and felt that Martin had lost a lot of credibility and respect.

In this example, Martin was either not aware of his emotions, or he failed to control them. He had no empathy with the team and was unaware of their feelings or their reactions to his behaviour.

New Manager – How it should be done

A little while later, Jane was promoted from within the same team to manager. She had an additional hurdle to cross as she now had to establish herself as the manager, having been a peer of her former teammates, some of whom also applied for the manager position.

Recognising that exerting her authority in a team meeting was not going to succeed, Jane chose to meet with each of the team individually first. She took time to acknowledge the views and feelings of each of the team members, in reaction to her appointment. She took particular care with her peers that had also applied for her position. She expressed her humility in not having all the answers and needing their support. She treated each of them with respect and acknowledged their years of experience. The reaction from each of the team members was relief that they had a manager who cared. They willingly offered their support and a good working relationship was quickly established.

In this case, Jane was successful because she displayed understanding and empathy, she understood that simply wielding her authority would be short sighted and that she needed to re-establish a personal connection with each of her former peers.

Exercise

Consider a recent interaction you have had. It may be one to one or in a group, it may be with a member of staff, a customer, a supplier, or may your manager. Score yourself (out of 10, 1 is low and 10 is high) against the 12 behaviours.

	Trait	Score
1	Awareness of your feelings	
2	Taking time to think before responding	
3	Awareness of your thinking style	
4	Questioning yourself – your thoughts and feelings	
5	Authenticity – were you true to your values?	
6	Did you demonstrate empathy and understanding?	
7	Did you demonstrate humility?	
8	If there was an opportunity to give feedback and praise – did you take it?	
9	Did you show forgiveness or atonement?	
10	Did ego or politics influence you?	

11	Were you open to new ideas and input?	
12	Were you constructive and look forward?	

Consider your scores and where the opportunities are for you to apply more emotional intelligence to your next interaction.

"If you are tuned out of your own emotions you will be poor at reading them in other people."
– Daniel Goleman

EI in the Workplace

Putting it into practice is not easy. It requires a conscious effort but every relationship, every interaction, provides an opportunity to develop and hone the techniques and behaviours of emotional intelligence.

Emotional intelligence can be developed, just with any other form of intelligence. But it requires a conscious effort and practise. There is no formula for managing situations with emotional intelligence but the following techniques can be used in many, if not all, situations. It may be a one to one discussion, either in a formal or informal setting. It may be a meeting with several attendees – regardless of your role. It may be an interaction with a customer, supplier, or another third party. In all cases it is an interaction between people, in a business context maybe, but still between people. And emotional intelligence will be a determining factor in how well it goes.

Successful leaders will develop their emotional intelligence and continue to do so throughout their careers. However, these are skills that every individual needs regardless of their role or position. We all have relationships in our professional lives as well as our personal lives. In a business context we are engaging with teams, customers, suppliers, managers, and so on. Whether it is a passing acquaintance, or a long-term professional relationship strong emotional intelligence will enable the relationship to be successful.

Self-awareness

You can examine your self-awareness at any time. In any given situation, ask yourself the following questions:

- What emotions am I feeling? These may change as discussions unfold, or information is provided, other factors come in to play. How are my emotions changing? In each case, ask why. What is causing me to feel the emotion I do? And, is it a reasonable emotion to be feeling? If you are getting frustrated or angry – is it with the person you are interacting with or the situation? Is it because of the impact to you personally or the impact to the business?

- Are you responding to a business issue on a personal level? For example, if you have to rework something you have already completed, or something has happened to cause you delay, it can be very frustrating, but if it is a genuine business issue, then it can be managed and responded to as such, and the emotion removed from the situation.

- As you interact with the person or people around you, ask: what effect am I having on them and their emotions? And why? How are they responding to what you are saying and how you are behaving? It may be that they have a low level of emotional intelligence and not responding as you would expect. Can you gauge this and adjust your conversation to suit?

You can also become aware of your body language, physiology, and stress levels. Are you relaxed and open to the discussion? Are you hunched up and feeling stress in your shoulders? Are you leaning forward and gritting your teeth? Become aware of the physical portrayal of your emotions and whether they too are creating the right impression and affect.

Self-control

- If you are aware of your emotions, are you able to control them? This may be a negative emotion such as disappointment or anger, where a lack of self-control can lead to an ill-considered, perhaps even unprofessional, response. It is easy to react in the heat of the moment. Being aware of rising emotions is critical to controlling them.

- This can equally apply to positive emotions such as excitement and enthusiasm. If you are presented with a great opportunity, it is easy to look at all the possibilities and focus on the best outcomes. But it this can easily lead to blinkered thinking and ignorance of the risks and downside. Be self-aware enough to know when this is happening and control the emotion to look at the situation objectively.

- Pause. We have all sent an email when we should have saved it and come back to it when we have had time to consider our response. Often this would result in a complete rewrite of the email to much greater effect. The same brake can be applied to any communication. If a face to face, telephone, text, online dialogue, is getting out of control, then take a break. Create a pause in the dialogue and time for all parties to reflect. This may mean taking time to 'sleep on it', i.e. allowing time for the emotions to subside, and our objective rational brain to review the situation.

- Self-control also means doing the right thing by the individual and company, so is your response the right one? Are you reacting to a situation with a short-term knee-jerk response? Or are you considering the long-term implications and what is right for the individual and the business? Test your thinking before you respond.

Motivation

- Test your motivation. Are you following your own personal agenda in any given situation, or that of the business? All of us act with an element of 'what's in it for me?' but part of this thinking needs to be upholding the highest standards. Taking an easy option because of short-term personal gain may often not be the right long-term solution. Ask is your motivation the right one?

- High performance leadership, applied with emotional intelligence, means you are just as concerned with the agenda of the person or people you are dealing with. In a business negotiation everyone will strive for a win–win solution, and the same applies to a personal interaction. A win–lose scenario will simply create a bigger problem for another day.

- Motivation increases with doing the right thing, not just for the business, but for the people around you. Notice how you feel when you have acknowledged and responded to someone's feelings, even if you cannot give them what they wanted – you will have demonstrated that you are trying, and perhaps constrained by things outside of your control. With that will come a level of satisfaction, and an increased motivation to understand and help others.

Empathy

To behave and respond with empathy you need to understand the emotions of other individuals and demonstrate that you understand.

- Listen to the other person. Really listen, pay attention, not just hear their words.

  If you are truly displaying empathy, and want to develop your emotional intelligence, then you will care enough about the other persons views to want to listen properly. You will give them 100% of your attention and not simply wait until your turn to speak.

  Read the body language, listen to their tone of voice, the speed they are talking, their facial expressions. They are all clues to their current emotions. Only 7% of communication is the words used (known as Mehrabian's rule following the research by Albert Mehrabian in 1967). Everything else makes up the rest. Notice how their emotions may be changing. How are they feeling? And why? What is causing them to feel this way? If you were in their position would you be feeling the same?

- Change the environment and ask again – if you want or need to dig deeper try changing the environment of the discussion. Informal discussions often give way to new information and different emotions. Discussions in a smaller group or one to one instead of a large meeting will have a similar effect. Listening to someone and understanding their emotions is not a one-time activity.

- Reflect what you are hearing. You can do this verbally, by playing back and testing your understanding, but you can also do this with your facial expressions and body language. If you are interacting with someone who is visibly upset, then you can demonstrate your understanding, and care, by your expressions, and how you sit or stand in relation to them. Reflecting back to the individual is just as important as understanding their feelings, because without it how would they know you understand?

Demonstrating empathy does not mean giving in to someone's demands, or giving them what they want to keep them happy. More often than not in a business context that will not be possible, or even the right thing to do. But by demonstrating empathy you are validating and recognising their right to have a view and an opinion. This will put you in a stronger position to continue discussions and support the individual.

Social skills

There are many other aspects to emotional intelligence that you can practice in group settings:

- Is there an opportunity to give praise? All too often these opportunities are only fleeting and get ignored yet praise and recognition is a basic human need that we all have, regardless of our achievements. Make a conscious effort to give praise where it is due and see what affect it has. Look out for these opportunities – and if missed make a note to do better next time, or if it is not too late – then make the effort to give the praise after the event.

- Meetings and group settings are a good opportunity to practise reading the room as well as the individuals in it. Most people can gauge the mood of a room fairly quickly, so ask yourself – where does it come from? Who is influencing it? how? Why? It may be that the mood of the room is directly connected with the discussion, but it may also be that it is incongruent and there are outside factors impacting the meeting. For example, bad news delivered in a previous meeting that has nothing to do with this one. By understanding the room, and the effect on and by individuals in the room, then it is possible to change it. Perhaps the audience is wrong, or the timing is wrong, or the communication is just not being delivered effectively. An emotionally intelligent leader will be able to detect this and make adjustments for it.

- Misunderstandings. Can you spot where a communication is breaking down? Perhaps the individuals involved are talking at cross purposes? Perhaps one or more of them is making an assumption and not aware of it? Perhaps they both have valid points but not recognising them with each other. Volume and temperatures can quickly rise as each party tries to 'win' the point. If you can see where the communication is flawed, and close the gap, then you can defuse the situation and emotions will quickly subside. If left unchecked the situation can go from bad to worse and become a major issue.

- Conflict resolution. In a business context an emotionally intelligent leader is required to resolve a conflict efficiently, with respect, and maintaining the dignity of all involved. This requires all the different facets of emotional intelligence – being self-aware enough, and with self-control, to not become embroiled in the conflict. To demonstrate empathy, not agreement, with the participants, and to motivate everyone to see and focus on the common objective that will provide the path to resolution. Of course, not all conflicts can be resolved and occasionally the result will be an agreement to disagree. This may result in the loss of a customer, or declining to do business with a supplier, but there is no reason why the conflict cannot be managed astutely, with emotional intelligence, and reach a resolution without emotional fall-out.

Authenticity

True emotional intelligence is genuine and authentic. Whilst it can be developed, and EI behaviours learnt and practised, it can only be effectively delivered with authenticity. Anything else will be recognised for what it is. Attempting to act with emotional intelligence, without an authentic desire and motivation, will ultimately fail but will also be seen to be disingenuous.

Developing Emotional Intelligence

Our emotional intelligence is an essential part of who we are. It reflects our ability to empathise with others as well as to understand and control our own emotions. It follows then that to develop emotional intelligence you have to be consciously aware of your level of emotional intelligence, your feelings, and how you think about things.

> *"Managing your impulsive, emotional chimp*
> *as an adult will be one of the biggest factors*
> *determining how successful you are in life."*
> – Dr Steve Peters

Our emotions are driven by the sensory input our brains receive. This input travels into our brains via the spinal cord and into our limbic brain (our emotional chimp) that generates our emotions. Only when the information passes to our Frontal Cortex does our adult rational brain have the opportunity to take control.

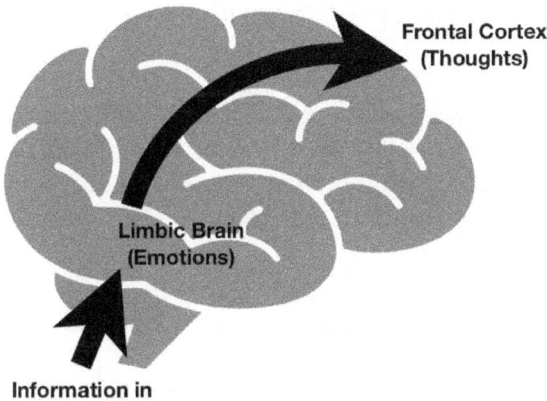

The dialogue between the adult rational brain and the emotional limbic brain is where emotional intelligence develops. By practicing emotional intelligence techniques, and repeating those behaviours until they become habit, we build the neurological connections that allow our inherent emotional intelligence to increase.

And it is a dialogue. If our emotional limbic brain is allowed to dominate then we will act according to our emotions, often responding inappropriately or making rash decisions. Only by engaging our adult rational brain can we examine our emotions, learn how to control them, and ensure we respond with objective rational thinking, and make the right decisions.

The most effective leaders have one common trait – they all have high emotional intelligence. They have many other skills and emotional intelligence alone does not make a leader, but to succeed in a leadership role emotional intelligence is essential. There are numerous research articles that have endorsed these findings (see Recommended Reading at the end of this book).

> *"No doubt, emotional intelligence is more rare than book smarts, but my experience says it is actually more important in the making of a leader."*
> – Jack Welch

7 Tips for building Emotional Intelligence

There are a multitude of ways to develop emotional intelligence and everyone will have their own preferences and things that work for them. In practice these are the things common to most published guidance and perceived wisdom:

1. Pick your words wisely
    Whoever you are communicating with, whether it be a friend, colleague, partners, family member, choose your words carefully. Consider the implications of the words you use and how they may be misinterpreted. Do they really convey what you mean to say? Are they too strong? Perhaps not strong enough? Are you communicating your thoughts and feelings, or attacking and criticising the other person? The vocabulary you use will and

how you deliver it will have an effect and will create a response – is it the one you really wanted?

2. Look after your body
   It is hard to avoid an emotional response and keep control of your thoughts and feelings if you are physically stressed. This includes being tired, hungry or dehydrated. If you are going into an important discussion, then make sure you are physically prepared and ready. Watch out for the warning signs and trust your instincts. If you are not in the right place physically or mentally to have a certain conversation, then reschedule it rather than risk it deteriorating and making matters worse.

3. Know your stressors
   Unless you are actively choosing to move outside of your comfort zone, know the situations or circumstances that cause stress or negative emotions, and take steps to avoid or minimise them. For example, if someone is a negative drain on your energy, then arrange to work with someone else, or delegate the interaction so someone else is dealing with the individual. This is not to avoid a problem or confrontation, but to manage your own time, emotions, and network.

4. Be alert to negative thinking
   There are many different negative thinking styles and we all use them sometimes. If something negative happens we will sometimes criticise ourselves with 'I should have…', or we will find someone else to blame and vent our thoughts on them. Or perhaps we will take something to an extreme and let a minor inconvenience become a major problem for us. Whatever the way of

thinking if it is negative and damaging then pause, stop, and turn the thinking around to something positive and constructive. Look forward not backwards.

5. Be open
    Be open in both senses of the word. Be open to new information, difference perspectives, and the views of others. Whatever the situation it is very likely with the additional input, perhaps after discussing it with others, that your views and thinking will evolve and change. Be open to this happening. But also be open to the person or people you are dealing with. If you can be honest with them and yourself then you will be acting with integrity, and quite possibly with empathy.

6. Watch for negative emotions
    We have all been in situations where we feel our 'blood start to boil', and our 'blood pressure' increase. These are the alarm bells that we are at risk of losing control. Identify what is causing this and take a different approach and if that fails then pause and take a break. Be aware of your emotions and use that information for your rational brain. What is it telling you?

7. Become resilient
    If you want to become more emotional intelligent, then you have to become more resilient. Developing your resilience, and managing your emotions when things have not gone your way, is a common scenario and opportunity to learn. If something has not worked out as you had hoped, or you have failed at something, then to manage the situation with emotional intelligence you have to develop your resilience and learn to cope and bounce back from the situation.

Exercise

Consider how you perform in each of the six areas and identify the opportunities you have in each case to bring more emotional intelligence to your next discussion with a key interaction.

1	Self-awareness
2	Self-control
3	Empathy
4	Motivation
5	Social Skills
6	Authenticity

Part 3:
Applying It

Is it just my imagination or do you get the feeling that not everyone is on board?

> *"Change is hard at first, messy in the middle,*
> *and gorgeous at the end."*
> – Robin Sharma

Psychology of Change

Change is fraught with emotion, even a change to our
plans for the day can give rise to extreme emotion.
Understanding the reasons why, how emotions can be
managed, and allowing our adult rational brains to
take over is key. But this is not enough – we have to
learn how to think positively and constructively.

This chapter is not intended to be an academic description of the psychology of change. There are many textbooks and other resources in existence that can provide a much more rigorous description. However, it is not possible to understand change, and therefore how to manage its effects, without a basic knowledge of how we react and respond to change, the emotions it generates, and why.

No discussion on change is complete without including the change curve which is probably the most well-known model. There are now many variations but the original model is attributed to Elisabeth Kübler-Ross. She first studied the impact of grief upon those that were dying or had just lost a loved one in the 1960s.

Many types of change, particularly negative change, involve the loss of something such as a job, current role, or current team, for example. This loss also creates a sense of grief or grieving in those that have suffered the loss. It also applies to change on a smaller scale. For example, if a planned leave is cancelled, we 'grieve' for what we have lost. It may be less significant and a shorter process but the model still applies. The model has since been developed and is now recognised to apply to many types of change. There are other models for change but for the purposes of this book we will use this one.

The change curve should not be read as linear progression. People move backwards and forwards through different emotions and progression is not as smooth as a curve suggests. The different variations may use different labels but all show the three distinct stages of the curve.

The diagram on the following page shows the curve with each of the distinct phases and stages of change. Any individual, depending on what else is going on in their lives, may be dealing with a number of changes and be in a different place on the curve for each change, but they will have a compounding affect.

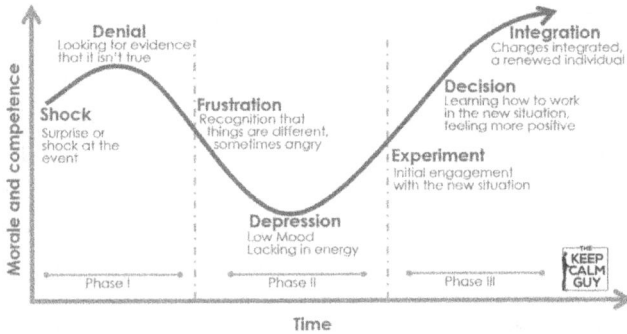

Change Curve

Stage 1: Shock & Denial

Shock

The first reaction to a trigger event. This does not always refer to a negative and could equally be surprise at a positive event. The shock or surprise may also be felt when an event is partially or even fully expected. For example; even if redundancies are expected the moment of actually losing a job will trigger an emotional reaction. That the event itself has taken place can generate this emotion and is often due to the timing being out of the control of the individual. It may be short-lived or not.

Shock is often accompanied by confusion and disbelief. When the event is totally unexpected it raises numerous questions. Questions that the mind seeks answers for to make sense of what has happened. At this point the mind may jump to the wrong answer or wrong conclusion.

Denial

Particularly with negative change it is human nature to cling to the past, with what was known, and probably comfortable. Denial looks for possibilities to avoid the change or even evidence that the trigger event is not true or could be undone. By definition it is a lack of acceptance and rejection of the event. For example, the speeding ticket arriving in the post. The first instinct is to question whether it is correct, even with photographic evidence. We check it and double check it looking for some evidence that it is wrong. At the back of our mind our rational brain knows that it is correct.

Stage 2: Anger/Frustration & Depression

Anger & Frustration

Frustration and even anger arise at the point where denial cannot continue. The realisation hits and the consequences of the change are faced. At this point we look for someone or something to blame. A target for our anger and frustration. We look at all the ways the change could have been avoided and ask 'why did I not?' At this point our rational brain knows that the question is pointless and the change cannot be undone.

Depression

As the frustration and anger fade away what is left is the absolute realisation of the change and its consequences. This is the lowest point emotionally when what has been lost must be faced. Focus is on the negative impact of the change. Not just what has been lost but also all the negative implications. Every minor point or irritation just adds to the sadness and depression.

Stage 3: Experiment, Decision, Integration

Experiment

At this point we start to move forwards towards acceptance. We look at ways to deal with the change. We look for options to work with the change and mitigate the consequences. For example, when a job is lost we look at other options and possibilities. With the speeding ticket example, we look for options to reduce the fine with early payment. There are often options and opportunities that we start to identify and explore. We start to feel positive about the possibilities. The more action we take the more in control we feel. Our rational brain starts to take over from the emotion and look at the change and its implications with clearer thinking.

Decision

We are now able to take action and steps to deal with the change. We may still feel regret that the change has occurred, but we recognise that it has happened, and we have to move forward. As we take these steps we have a greater feeling of control and with control we feel more positive about the future. As we explore possibilities and opportunities, we are able to identify positive aspects and as we do so we move towards acceptance.

Reactions & Responses

When a trigger event or change situation arises it often feels like our immediate response is an emotional one – as the labels in the change curve imply. However, this is preceded by our thoughts and interpretation of the event and situation. We almost instantly jump to a conclusion regarding the impact of the event and its consequences. This then leads to our emotional response as shown in the diagram below. This usually happens so quickly that our emotions become tightly coupled to the change event itself and we associate one with the other.

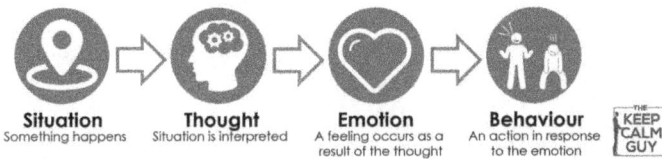

Situation Something happens ⇨ **Thought** Situation is interpreted ⇨ **Emotion** A feeling occurs as a result of the thought ⇨ **Behaviour** An action in response to the emotion

THE KEEP CALM GUY

We will often then take action as a result of our emotions, even if that is not the best time to decide how to react and proceed. Depending on the action we take it may change the situation or lead to another event or situation. This in turn will lead to another reaction and potentially a whole cycle of events.

As an example, let's look at someone facing an office relocation to somewhere less convenient. The thought process will be of longer commute times and costs, and this may lead to feelings of frustration, despondency, possibly anger. The whole change process in relation to the relocation could potentially lead to options such as a number of different travel options, and possibly even opportunities such as car-sharing or home working. However if the behaviour and next action taken is to reject the change and to start applying for new positions, either inside or outside the business, then that will lead to a whole new change curve, This cycle is sometimes referred to as the 'think feel do' cycle.

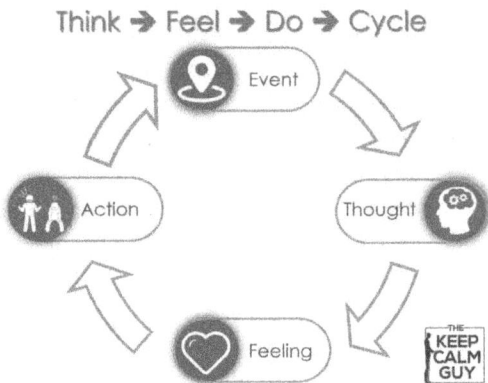

Think ➜ Feel ➜ Do ➜ Cycle

Managing change, and the reactions and responses of staff, particularly across a team of people who may all respond differently, needs great skill and care. The emotional intelligence of the manager and leader in this situation will determine how successful the outcome is, whether the change is accepted and adopted with ease, or whether there is significant resistance.

*"The secret of change is to focus your energy,
not on fighting the old, but on building the new."*
— Socrates

Leading Change with EI

*Employing emotional intelligence requires a
conscious effort, even for experienced leaders.*

All change in a business ultimately has to be made by the people in it. The initiative and direction may have come from the top, but executing the change effectively will come down to the people, their relationships, and the meetings and conversations they hold to discuss and accept (or not) the change.

Like all critical discussions, a little time spent on planning and preparing for it, applying the skills of EI, will be time well spent. Consider the following points as you prepare for your next key discussion:

- Are you clear on the objective of the discussion? If so, how will you ensure the other person shares your expectation? This does not mean that you necessarily reach your desired outcome, but that you both have a common objective for the discussion.

- Are you mentally and emotionally ready for the discussion? i.e. are you in the right frame of mind or right mood? If not, be prepared to reschedule it.

- Are you open to new information or the discussion going in directions other than you have planned? i.e. you are not blinkered and fixated on one outcome. Have you anticipated the questions, possibly some you do not have the answer to? How will you handle them?

- How will you use your emotional intelligence to manage the discussion with humanity and integrity? See below.

Every discussion is unique as the individuals involved, but the following 8 techniques can be applied in every case. As well as ensuring a successful discussion, they will also help the development of emotional intelligence and good habits:

1. **Remember the person** – empathy starts with the ability to see things through the eyes or another, from their perspective. Before you enter the discussion consider the position of the other person or people, their perspectives, from a personal level, not just a professional one. Look beyond the job description or job title, look at the individual.

2. **Integrity first** – communicate with honesty, openness, and fairness. Treat people as you would expect to be treated. Truth and respect will be reciprocated. Remember you are having a business discussion about a business issue. It is not personal and you can manage it fairly and objectively.

3. **Listen** – listen fully and completely. Show the other person the respect of paying attention and not being distracted by a phone or email. Listen fully to what the other person is saying, listen to their body language, listen to what they are not saying. If you find yourself thinking about how you will respond, pause, and make sure you have heard what the other person is saying.

4. **Reflect** – listening with empathy will be lost if your understanding is not reflected back to the individual. Reflection is not just for your benefit – to confirm your understanding – but also the individual to demonstrate you have listened and understood. This does not mean you agree with their views but you have heard them.

5. **Do the right thing** – there are three perspectives to consider. Do the right thing by the individual, by yourself and your role, and the business. There may be different needs and wants, but by taking a 'big picture'

view and long-term solution perspective, the right thing to do, or the right options, will become clear. It should be possible to articulate a common goal or objective.

6. **Stay in control** – watch your own feelings and responses during the discussion and be aware if your own emotions start to run high. If necessary, pause the discussion and come back to it another time.

7. **Move forward** – ultimately the discussion will have to move toward looking at options, solutions, and the way forward. Allow time for views to be shared and input given, but make sure the conversation is steered towards looking at the future, rather than the past.

8. **Stay open** – be prepared for new information to be provided, and if you do not understand the responses you are getting, or the reasons why, then probe and ask questions. Do not avoid or dismiss issues or concerns that may be raised. Be open to the fact that concerns raised may be understated, or the other person is being overly diplomatic. Their comments may mask strong feelings or a more serious issue.

CASE STUDY

This case study is a real-life example of an internal negotiation. The solution to many business issues is often a negotiation and agreement over the solution. Again, the names have been changed.

Negotiation – How not to do it

John needed to speak to the manager of another department, Sam, to get his agreement to provide a number of critical resources to John's project. He knew this would be a difficult conversation – Sam was under a lot of pressure from other customers and short of resources.

John felt he had to make sure his voice was heard, and that 'he who shouts loudest' will be heard. He was also expected by his (internal) customer to campaign for the resources he needed and not let his project suffer.

The meeting did not start well. Sam knew what was coming and when John started laying down his demands, he put up the barriers to defend himself from the added pressure. John got frustrated at not making progress, and the tension between John and Sam was palpable. Sam made a note of John's request, but eventually John left empty handed. John was disappointed, and Sam was getting angry at the demands he had to deal with.

In this case, John approached the meeting with the single objective of getting his demands met, and when this did not happen his emotions started to rise and he felt he had to make his case stronger. In response Sam dug his heels in further and became more vehement in his response.

Negotiation – How it should be done

Mary had to approach Sam with the same request for her project. Before meeting with Sam she considered the situation and the pressure that Sam must be under. She considered her own objective (getting resources for her project), and put this in the context of Sam's objective (providing resources to multiple projects).

The meeting started with Mary summarising her needs, without making demands of Sam. Sam responded by explaining his situation and the constraints he was working within, with Mary acknowledged. They then had a discussion about the options, with neither side becoming emotional, the conversation remained rational and objective. The meeting concluded with Sam committing to explore one particular option and to get back to Mary. She did this and allocated the resources that Mary needed.

In this case, Mary acknowledged the pressure that Sam was under (demonstrated empathy), and kept her emotions under control when not immediately having her demands met. In response, Sam showed understanding towards Mary, and they worked together to find a solution.

"Wherever there is a human being,
there is an opportunity for kindness."
– Seneca

Beyond EI

Development emotional intelligence and
understanding the psychology of change may not
be enough. We all need support sometimes.

There are two sides to any interaction, so let us look at two scenarios. Firstly, where a staff member does not have the emotional intelligence to deal and respond to a situation rationally. In this case even a manager with high levels of emotional intelligence will need to make additional allowances and consider other strategies.

Secondly, we will look at a manager or leader who is still learning and building experience of leading individuals and teams, and also building their emotional intelligence. In most organisations the majority of staff are managed by the first line of management. These are often people that are promoted in to their first line management role and therefore do not have all the skills and experience to deal with potentially difficult situations, such as implementing organisational change. In this case we have the most junior levels of management attempting to execute a critical business change, and they will need support.

Struggling Staff Member

Even with a highly experienced leader with high levels of emotional intelligence, there will still be times when the staff member struggles to accept the change. This can sometimes be viewed as a refusal to accept change and will tempt the manager to take a hard line. There is a fine line to tread between making allowances to the individual, and driving the business change through regardless of the consequences. A balance has to be struck between giving time and additional support to the individual, possibly even making compromises, and enforcing the business change accepting this may be at the cost of demotivating and possibly losing the individual. Managing the situation with emotional intelligence, but also with integrity, means doing the right thing by the individual, as well as the business, and if managed correctly these do not need to be mutually exclusive.

The first aspect to consider is the moral and legal duty of care. Obviously there is a legal responsibility which should underpin all discussions and actions taken. But there is also a moral duty that will be felt acutely by the individual as well as the manager (if he or she is acting with integrity). Some would argue that there is not room for this additional layer of care and attention, and that the time and effort it requires is not necessary. The CEO and Executive team may feel that they have to take a hard line and force change through, this may even have become part of the company culture. However, this is short-sighted and a short-term solution (and they may recognise and accept this).

A leadership team acting with integrity will do the right thing by the individual and put additional support in place. Even if they cannot see this, they will recognise that how the individual is supported, or not, will impact their reputation as an employer, a reputation that will last long after the change project has completed.

Without the right support an individual may feel unfairly treated, and that their situation is unjust. An emotionally intelligent leader will have empathy with the individual and will avoid this situation arising.

In all cases it is essential to identify a common objective – whether or not it can be met with a mutually acceptable solution. If a common objective can be found then there is an agreement, and this can be the starting point for looking at options and possible solutions. The emotionally intelligent approach is to find the common ground and work from there. For example, in the case of relocation it may be agreement that there is insufficient office space. In the case of a team restructure it may be agreement that the team is over-resourced in some areas and under-resourced in others. Whatever the circumstance it is usually possible to work back and find a common objective to agree on, before then working forward.

When a common objective has been found, this provides an opportunity to work tougher to find a solution, or at least give the individual an opportunity to give input and contribute. This will allow him or her to feel that you are working collaboratively even if the ultimate decision is with the manager.

Recognise where the individual is on the change curve and give them reasonable time to progress through it. All too often the manager will be involved in the change planning many weeks or months before the individual. The manager will have had time to adapt to the change and progress through the change curve personally. He or she will be at a point of accepting the change but the individual will be at the start of the journey and will need time to process and adjust.

In some cases, external support may be needed or beneficial to help work through the change. This could be career counselling, mediation, or coaching and mentoring – possibly for both the individual and manager.

In the next chapter we will look at the second scenario, providing support to managers and leaders who are on the front line of implementing change.

*"A leader can be very destructive or inspiring,
it comes down to their level of emotional intelligence."*
– John Mackey

Leadership Support

Leaders at all levels will need support and coaching to make change with emotional intelligence. Increasingly the value of taking care of employees, so that they will take care of customers, is becoming widely recognised. For this to become embedded in the culture of a business it has to come from the top. Junior Management has the least amount of experience, but sometimes the senior leadership team has the greatest need for coaching and support.

A leader with emotional intelligence will be able to show humility. This is a sign of confidence and strength, rather than a weakness. As a manager or leader there is a false perception that they have to be right – in every situation and circumstance. Yet this is clearly not possible – even the greatest of leaders, via their humility, will admit there are gaps in their knowledge, skills they are not very good at, and times when they welcome the advice and coaching of others.

Every manager and leader in an organisation, from the most junior, to the seasoned CEO or Executive will also have gaps and weaknesses in their emotional intelligence – and recognising this is a strength and opportunity. Blind denial is ignorance and naivety. Where and how can managers and leaders be supported in developing their emotional intelligence? Everyone is at a different stage of their management career path and building the relevant emotional intelligent skills they need. To answer this question let us look at the following distinct groups.

First Line Management

Someone in their first line management roles faces a particularly tough challenge. They are new to the role, and new to being a manager – so even if they have the right functional experience they are a complete novice at managing a team of people. If they have been promoted from within the team they face the added challenge of establishing new relationships with their former peers – some of who may not be happy with the appointment. All of this gives rise to the following areas of challenge where support may be needed:

1. Staff management training: It is not enough simply to brief them on the company processes and their role within them. These are simply mechanisms for handling routine events. The relationship between a line manager and his or her staff members is the biggest factor in satisfaction of that staff member, and therefore their engagement and productivity. A new manager needs to be equipped and supported with the skills necessary to establish a relationship with the individual based on respect and trust. This can only be built over time and a manager left without the right support is likely to make many avoidable mistakes.

    Putting in place a training programme that will build their emotional intelligence and leadership behaviours, above and beyond the responsibilities of their role, will ensure they grow into successful leaders.

2. A manager promoted from within a team (at any level) faces the added challenge of establishing new relationship with former peers. Their response will, in part, be a reflection of their emotional intelligence. Regardless, the new manager will need to adapt and respond to each individual to establish new boundaries and expectations. If this is not handled effectively the relationship could deteriorate and become and on-going problem for the manager, and the whole team. A disgruntled team member can have a negative effect on those around them. This in turn will simply make the challenge of the new manager even greater, and possibly reach the point of being insurmountable.

3. A junior manager will repeatedly encounter new situations over a number of months and years until they have built a

suitable level of experience and developed a range of skills to cope with those situations. During this time a mentor with a high level of emotional intelligence, as well as experience, is essential to the development of the manager.

CEO & Executive Team

Ultimately the responsibility for leading an organisation is with the CEO and Executive team. This means the CEO, and the team, <u>will</u> lead by example, regardless of what they may say. If a CEO cannot lead with emotional intelligence, and all the behaviours that includes, then the relationship with executive team will not be a successful one. Unless it is an exceptionally strong team (in which case they will not tolerate a weak CEO), at least some of the team will replicate the behaviour of the CEO and consider that to be what is expected of them.

Similarly, if the Executive team do not possess sufficient emotional intelligence they will not act as a team, nor will they set the right example to their teams.

At the most senior levels in any organisation the responsibility to act with decisiveness, clarity, and commitment is immense. The perceived need to be seen as a strong leader, by clearly ambitious people, often in the face of competitive political pressures, leaves no room for doubt, or uncertainty. This directly conflicts with the nature of someone with high emotional intelligence who will listen and understand the point of view, and feelings, of others. Changing the culture of an executive team such that they act as a team, requires a strong CEO to not only demonstrate the behaviours expected, but also to not tolerate anything less.

Senior and Middle Management

Middle and senior levels of management have the challenge of operational responsibility for running the business as directed by the Executive team, but also managing and supporting their own management teams and resources. They have to follow the strategy and vision laid down the Executive team and interpret this and put it into operational practice with their teams.

These levels of management are often where the tension arises between the business strategies and vision, and the realities of implementing them. Inevitably there are unforeseen difficulties and issues fed back by Junior Management and their staff. These need to be listened to and understood, before judgement is made on the way forward.

When making changes to the business, this could be everything from delivering performance reviews, to a complete restructure, the Middle and Senior Management teams may be caught between seemingly fixed constraints imposed by the Executive team, and the realities of implementing them. They require all their man management skills and emotional intelligence to both support their management teams and progress with the changes. They also require support, direction, coaching, and mentorship from their superiors.

Part 4:
The Way Forward

Here at WIBLINGS we believe in treating all our staff as individuals, you will be individual No. 675–67c

"Letters are expectation packaged in an envelope."
– Shana Alexander

A Letter to You

You may be reading this book as a leader making change in his or her business, as a manager responsible for making the change, or a team member struggling with what you are being asked to do. Here are my thoughts on your position.

Letter to the CEO

Dear CEO,

If you are reading this letter, then you already know that integrity and emotional intelligence are crucial for anyone interested in their role and their business for the long term. No matter what pressures you are currently under, you will know that ultimately it is the people in the business that make it work and the hearts and minds of the people can so easily be lost.

More than this, you know that like you, they are so much more than the role they perform for you. They are people with hopes and dreams, worries and fears. They are husbands, wives, mothers, and fathers. Only by treating them as people rather than resources, by showing that you care, will they care. Only be treating them with respect will they show you respect. Only by demonstrating loyalty to them, will the give it to you.

This is not to negate the challenges the business is facing, difficult decisions that may have to be made, and the need for objective dispassionate thinking that may require. But these things are not mutually exclusive – tough leadership can also be made with empathy and understanding, as the most successful leaders are able to do.

Please, use this letter to consider what more you can do to lead by example, and show your team how you expect them to operate, what it means to live your values, to walk the talk.

If I can help in any way, just let me know.

Yours sincerely,

Bill.

Letter to the Leader

Dear Leader,

I am sure you prefer to be considered a leader rather than a manager. You understand the difference, and the value of having people follow you as a leader, rather than simply work for you as a manager. You understand the difference this means to the performance of your team, and the team's success – including your own.

Much has been written about leadership vs management, but all the books and articles on this subject have one thing in common. The thread running through management is task-focused and transactional. It is about getting the job done. The thread running through leadership is people, inspiring people, caring, supporting, and creating the right culture. It is about the team – the people.

By definition, you cannot lead without emotional intelligence. You need to connect with each person as an individual, and yes that means treating them each differently – they are unique. How well do you know them? Not as a job description, not as a role, not the results of their last appraisal. How will do you know the individual?

To truly lead, understand each team member, understand the relationship between you, and the relationship between team members. How well do they understand each other? How well do the understand your vision and have they really bought in to it? Is it aligned with their personal ambitions? More importantly, are they happy? Are you? If it is truly a team, then it matters and everyone will care.

If I can help you become a higher performing leader, and your team reach new heights of success, then just let me know.

Yours sincerely,

Bill.

Letter to the Team

Dear Team,

I don't know what challenges you are facing right now, and what changes the business is going through, but I guess you have a lot of unanswered questions. It may be an uncertain time, and an unsettling one. It may also be that the answers don't yet exist to all your questions.

Change can be difficult to deal with. The change curve and the emotions that go with it are well documented. Fortunately, there are many tools and techniques that can help you to understand the emotions you may be going through, how can understand where they have come from and thereby change them by changing your thinking. You can also change move away from the negative thoughts that may be dominating you at the moment, and adopt a more positive mindset that will help accept the changes and move forward. It isn't necessarily easy but it can be done. You will get through these changes and if you would like an insight in to how you can do this with less pain and more progress then read my book *How To Keep Calm and Carry On* – this is a very personal account of adjusting to change.

Be aware of your team, including your manager, and what these changes mean to them. No matter what the outward appearance, change is unsettling for everyone. Ultimately change within the business is being made for the right long-term reasons, even if the immediate consequences are unpalatable.

If I can assist your team, or even you on a one to one basis, then please do not hesitate to let me know.

I wish you all the best,

Bill.

"Act as if what you do makes a difference, it does."
– William James

The Real Transformation

The real change for a business is not the organisational one you may be facing at the moment, it is to transform your business and its leadership to one that inspires its people to follow it wherever it needs to go, by treating people with authenticity, integrity, and above all as people – not resources.

Emotional intelligence is the difference that makes the difference. When the leadership and management of any business applies emotional intelligence to <u>all</u> relationships then it is truly transformed. When emotional intelligence is valued as highly, if not more so, than any other form of skill, knowledge, or academic and technical intelligence, then the right people will be recruited. Politics, and egos will be all but eliminated, poor behaviour that does not uphold the values of the business will not be tolerated, and the business will perform at a level never before achieved.

Every interaction between team members will be supportive and constructive and true to the aims of the team, every conversation between a line manager and staff member will be completed with mutual trust and respect, every conversation with suppliers and partners will be aligned with a win–win result, and every discussion with customers will be focus on a common objective and generate trust and loyalty.

When the people in a business operate on this basis then it is truly transformed. Imagine what it would be like to work with or for an organisation where people were treated this way. It would foster huge levels of loyalty with staff, customers, and suppliers, it would be <u>the</u> place to work, business challenges would be faced with complete unity and determination, successes and achievements would be shared and celebrated by all, but most of all it would be fun. People would enjoy it. They would be happy to get out of bed in the morning and come to work.

More and more organisations are recognising the value of emotional intelligence and making this a key criterium for recruitment. Hard skills can be taught, but soft skills, and the emotional intelligence needed to develop them, are not always present. In the 21st century, as businesses are increasingly reliant on technology, artificial intelligence, and robotics, traditional technical and operational skills are becoming more and more commoditised. Emotional intelligence is increasingly becoming the lifeblood of an organisation – as this is what makes the interaction between people, whether it be staff, customers, or suppliers, work effectively.

To requote the *Harvard Business Review*: 'The most effective leaders are all alike in one crucial way, they all have a high degree of … emotional intelligence'. Recognising the value of emotional intelligence, creating the right culture to foster it within an organisation, and leading by example has to come from the top. It cannot be delegated or assigned to a management team – that makes in disingenuous and will fail at the first hurdle. By applying emotional intelligence within the executive team and expecting nothing less from their staff will begin the process of transformation.

Making this change will be a journey, a continuous one. Every individual in an organisation has a role to play and some will adapt to it easier than others. Some will become natural leaders and their integrity and values will shine, others will learn from the examples they are shown, and learn what is expected, and what is not acceptable behaviour. The business will evolve and grow in more ways than one.

"Action is the foundation key to all success."
– Pablo Picasso

Next Steps

Just take one thing from this book, and apply it to one relationship, and start to increase your emotional intelligence. Take several key points, and apply them to the most important relationships your life today, and they will be transformative.

Now that you understand the huge opportunity that exists in building the currency of emotional intelligence in any organisation, it is time to consider your own position, and your relationships with those you interact with on a daily basis.

Start by considering your own level of emotional intelligence, the behaviours you exhibit, and where you can develop. Think about how you behave in extreme situations. How do you react to bad news? How do you behave if you are delayed or someone is late meeting you? When are your emotions often running high or out of control? It is often helpful to get a different perspective on this and ask others what they think of your response in the same situations.

The Johari window is a good tool for comparing and contrasting how you see your behaviour with that of others. Use a real or hypothetical situation that would increase stress and possibly lead to an emotional response, and consider how you typically respond. Ask others to provide feedback on the same situations.

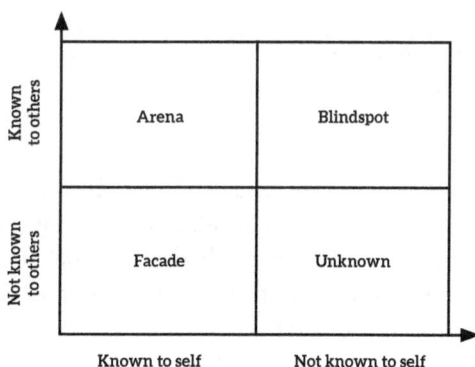

Johari window

Next, consider the people you interact with on a regular basis. This could be staff members, your leadership, suppliers, customers, or third parties. Start by considering the relationship that are most important to you by completing a stakeholder map, for example, and prioritising the relationships to focus on.

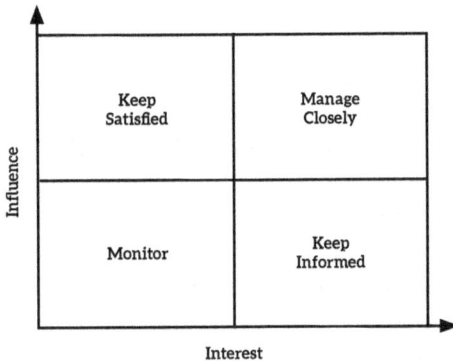

Stakeholder map

Next consider your own personality type, and that of each of the individuals you deal with. In some cases, there will be a good match and a working relationship that comes naturally, with others it will conflict and the relationship seem to be always tense and difficult. If you have not previously completed it consider doing the 4-colour personality profile, or Myers–Briggs profile. Both will help you understand your personality type and preferred methods of communication.

Make a list of the most important relationships in your business life and the opportunity you have for approaching the relationship with a higher level of emotional intelligence, and make a note in each case of which aspect you can address.

	Name	Notes
1		
2		
3		
4		
5		
6		

Finally, emotional intelligence is not just about making an effort with selected individuals for personal benefit, it is about approaching all relationships, no matter how fleeting, with the same level of integrity and authenticity.

"Calmness is the cradle of power."
– Josiah Gilbert Holland

The Keep Calm Guy

The Keep Calm Guy and Associates bring calmness and control to connect desired change with the hearts and minds of people involved.

In every industry, organisations are embarking on change and transformation programmes with the usual focus on change management. These skills and processes are essential but not sufficient. Even where external consultants are providing support and advice the focus is on the organisational design and mechanics of the change. In all cases there is a chasm between the direction of the leadership team and the emotional engagement of the people in the organisation.

The Keep Calm Guy and associates have been helping individuals, teams, and businesses bridge this gap and help people not only adapt to and accept the change, but learn to embrace it and the opportunities it holds. This is done via specific tailored services to suit the business:

- **Embracing Change**: One to one support for individuals facing change and perhaps unsure or struggling. This 5-step programme will help them face the future with confidence, and learn how to embrace the opportunities it may bring – even if they are not obvious at the moment. It will turn an anxious resource unsure of their future, back to a high performing staff member fully engaged with the change.

- **High Performing Emotionally Intelligent Teams**: Working with teams, departments or just groups of individuals, this programme will help people bring 100% of themselves to work – as individuals, not as job descriptions. By recognising that everyone is unique, and each has their own strengths to apply they can operate with confidence and integrity. They can focus on what they do best and bring more value to their role.

- **Lead with Emotional Intelligence**: Training and workshops for leadership teams at all levels. This bespoke programme will develop the thinking and feeling behind emotional intelligence and provide the techniques to build and enhance emotional intelligence in those that need to demonstrate it most.

  This is a bespoke programme that will target individual levels of leadership and equip them to overcome specific challenges.

Contact The Keep Calm Guy to discuss how we can help you and your business make change with the full engagement of your most precious asset – your people.

www.thekeepcalmguy.co.uk

email: hello@thekeepcalmguy.co.uk

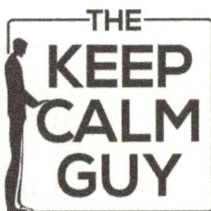

Recommend Reading

The Chimp Paradox – Dr Steve Peters, published by Vermilion.

How to Keep Calm and Carry On – Bill Mann, published by Austin Macauley.

The Dip – Seth Godin, Published by Piatkus Books.

Emotional Intelligence 2.0 – Travis Bradberry & Jean Greaves, published by TalentSmart.

TED Talk transcript: Jim Hemerling '5 ways to lead in an era of constant change'

Harvard Business Review, April 2015: "How Emotional Intelligence Became a Key Leadership Skill" – and associated articles.

The Idiot Brain – Dean Burnett, published by Guardian Faber Publishing.

About the Author

Bill Mann was born and raised in Essex. From school he went to the University of Surrey to study Mathematics and Computer Science. It was there that he made the decision to make a career in Information Technology and joined a global software house as a graduate programmer. After several years in various technical roles he ultimately made the decision to follow a management career path. He held several senior positions in a variety of organisations, finally ending up as Senior Vice President in a global financial services company.

As well as the software company, during his career Bill has worked for a global hardware manufacturer, a small UK boutique consultancy, an Australian bank, a European network company, a US-based software product company, and a global financial services organisation, amongst others. He has seen business change from every perspective – a merger, an acquisition, joint venture, and local and global restructuring. He has seen countless re-organisations, transformation programmes, recruitments, promotions, redundancies, terminations, pay reviews, and so on.

It was during his last role that Bill was caught up in the London bombings on 7th July 2005, and then lost his wife a few short years later. Following these events Bill left the corporate world and set up his own business. He now provides Executive Coaching to individuals and businesses specialising in embracing change, and leading change, with humanity and emotional intelligence. He described his personal experiences, and how he dealt with the life change events, in his first book: *How to Keep Calm and Carry On.*

Bill still lives in Essex with his new wife, and their children.

Acknowledgements

Many thanks to the very talented Fran Orford, Cartoonist, for creating the cartoons for each section. I am extremely grateful to Cathryn Hindle, an exceptional HR Director and Executive Coach, for her input, ideas, suggestions, and support.

Thank you to my wife, Sarah, for a number of the diagrams, and her input and ideas.

I would also like to thank my colleagues past and present. I have learnt something from all of them and collectively they have shaped my thinking.